Life Almost Faked Them Out

Destiny

Life Almost Faked Them Out

Destiny

VICTORIA ROBERTSON

Copyright © 2024 **Diane Rodriguez-Burton**

All rights reserved. No part of this publication may be reproduced, distributed, or transmitted in any form or by any means, including photocopying, recording, or other electronic or mechanical methods, without the prior written permission of the publisher, except in the case of brief quotations embodied in critical reviews and certain other noncommercial uses permitted by copyright law. For permission requests, write to the publisher, addressed "Attention: Book Rights and Permission," at the address below.

Published in the United States of America

ISBN 978-1-962730-74-7 (SC)
ISBN 979-8-89395-018-2 (HC)
ISBN 979-8-89395-017-5 (Ebook)

Library of Congress Control Number: 2024921062

Diane Rodriguez-Burton
222 West 6th Street
Suite 400, San Pedro, CA, 90731
www.stellarliterary.com

Ordering Information and Rights Permission:

Quantity sales. Special discounts might be available on quantity purchases by corporations, associations, and others. For details, contact the publisher at the address above.

For Book Rights Adaptation and other Rights Permission. Call us at toll-free 1-888-945-8513 or send us an email at admin@stellarliterary.com.

Contents

Dedication vi
Preface viii

The Excitement and Awkwardness of a First Relationship 1
Anticipation Jitters, Yikes! 4
The Question is, Will You Be My Girl? 6
Preparing for the Cotillion 9
Oh My Goodness, What Have We Done? 13
Professing a Love That Stood the Challenges of High School 19
Pressure Does Not Feel Good and Causes Irrational Behavior 23
When Dreams Change and Directions Differ, Two Cannot Walk in Agreement 27
Embracing One's Purpose Equals Success, but What About Getting Closure? 32
Release is Not Always Instantaneous, Is It? 35
Ghosts Can Haunt Us Sometimes When What We Need is Quiet Relief ... 41
From the Desk of the Author 50
About The Author 56

Dedication

I dedicate this book first to God for giving me the courage to write it. He has given us all stories that are woven around our purpose, whether we choose to live a life that fulfills it or not. Our true purpose is to love, even though we don't know how much time we have. Life is filled with many options and so many people that it is sometimes hard to know which to choose and who actually to listen to. I'm grateful, and I thank God for placing some recognizably wise people in my life who encourage me to make good choices. I would also like to dedicate this work to my dear friend and wise counselor, Pastor Diane Rodriguez-Burton.

Pastor Diane Rodriguez-Burton encouraged me by reminding me that the Lord gives everyone talents and gifts, and I inquired, what will I do with mine? Many have chosen to follow their hearts and use those gifts, while many have wasted their talents or procrastinated, not allowing their gifts ever to realize fruition. Pastor Diane is a no-nonsense and straightforward person whom I admire and respect.

I realized it even more as she said to me, "Victoria, the cemetery houses the bodies of countless numbers of untold stories, poems, prose, recipes, written pieces of great and vast literary varieties, and countless numbers of inventions and creative ideas. You need to do this so the grave will not bury this one. I am here to edit what you've written and encourage you throughout this powerful project." I had to agree as I also thought someone could be entertained, influenced, and even learn something from what I have to say that will have a life-changing effect on their life.

Pastor Diane said, very pointedly, "God has gifted you to use your talents and soar! Don't let them be unrealized and buried like so many other could've, should've, and would've souls who missed out on great opportunities because they failed to act upon them! You're better than that, and slothfulness is a sin!"

Author Elmer Towns explains that "the idea of 'to whom much is given, much will be required' is that we are held responsible for what we have. If we are blessed with talents, wealth, knowledge, time, and the like, we are expected to use these well to glorify God and benefit others."

I thank you so very much, Pastor Diane, for your encouragement and for listening to me, editing my work, and showing excitement about my creative ability and the building of this literary project.

Preface

"But he that knew not, and did commit things worthy of stripes, shall be beaten with few stripes. For unto whomsoever much is given, of him shall be much required: and to whom men have committed much, of him they will ask the more.

From everyone who has been given much, much will be required; and from him who has been entrusted with much, even more will be demanded."

(Luke 12:28, 48 KJV)

The aftermath and far reach for the spiritual resolve of a seemingly unfulfilled existence can cause prolonged and inexplicable grief. It is in the complete acceptance of humanity's biggest certainty, death that one will start to acknowledge it as part of life and, in doing so, come back to life.

Life almost faked them out! Hosea and India may never have had a successful life together on this plane due to their extreme differences in callings, their actual purposes, and overall life's expectancies, desires, and dreams. Yet they had a love as real as Romeo and Juliet's. A woman by the name of Jeanette Winterson was onto something that hinges on authenticity ("real talk") as she penned the following quote in a book called Written on the Body:

"You'll get over it…" It's the clichés that cause the trouble. To lose someone you love is to alter your life forever. You don't get over it because 'it' is the person you love. The pain stops; there are new people, but the gap never closes. How could it? The particularness of someone who mattered enough to grieve over is not made anodyne by death. This hole in my heart is in the shape of you, and no one else can fit it. Why would I want them to?"

As nice and genuinely sweet as he was and as much as I craved his unmatchable sweetness, I knew somehow, at some point in our newly acquired long-distance relationship existence, we were not destined to have the future we had planned out as teenagers together.

Our plans involved being together because we loved each other and allowed spontaneity to guide our daily and lifetime sustainment.

Dreams born from my early childhood purity, which I believed in and had spoken out loudly into the atmosphere around me, would somehow overshadow my current plans and become my reality. These were dreams that I had always envisioned would be fulfilled by God. As a young child, I was taught to dream big, live by faith, and believe in God's faithfulness and the fulfillment of what He had placed in me. How seemingly large and grand were my early childhood dreams long before I knew that an external love would someday develop and capture my innocent heart! Ultimately, I chose to live a life that enabled me to satisfy personal goals and natural desires to fulfill a purpose, destiny, and the abundant life Christ Jesus designed just for me. Anyone who accepts His gift of salvation has a purpose and future according to the plan for their life.

"For I know the plans I have for you," declares the Lord, "plans to prosper you and not to harm you, plans to give you hope and a future…" **(Jeremiah 29:11)**

I sorely mourned the thought that Hosea had missed a life mirroring the fulfillment I was blessed to grasp and continue to enjoy while living out my purpose. He was the love of my life, and since I truly loved him, I wanted him to live a long and fulfilled life, with or without me. I am sure that that's part of what real love looks like!

If I have the gift of prophecy and can fathom all mysteries and all knowledge, and if I have a faith that can move mountains, but do not have love, I am nothing. If I give all I possess to the poor and give over my body to hardship that I may boast, but do not have love, I gain nothing. Love is patient, love is kind. It does not envy, it does not boast, it is not proud. It does not dishonor others, it is not self-seeking, it is not easily angered, it keeps no record of wrongs. Love does not delight in evil but rejoices with the truth. It always protects, always trusts, always hopes, always perseveres. Love never fails.

"But where there are prophecies, they will cease; where there are tongues, they will be stilled; where there is knowledge, it will pass away."

— **(1 Corinthians 13:2–8)**

The Excitement and Awkwardness of a First Relationship

India Banks and Hosea Rivera were both from Macon, Georgia and came to know each other through a mutual acquaintance. My name is India Banks, and Hosea and I were fourteen-year-old high school students who attended rival schools in different sections of the city. I was a majorette at Central High School, and Hosea was a member of the marching band at McKendry Westside High School. George, our acquaintance, attended my school and had Mass at the same Catholic Church as Hosea. He and Hosea were looking through the current Central High yearbook when Hosea noticed my photo and inquired about me since he thought I was very attractive. Hosea gave George a picture of himself to take to school so he could share it with me and tell me he was interested in meeting me someday. He requested a phone number to reach out to me. After viewing his photo, I passed my number on and warned George that my brothers would beat him up if it were him instead of Hosea on the other end of the phone. After a couple of days, Hosea called. We both seemed very shy over the phone, but after the awkwardness had passed, we gelled and developed an excellent telephone relationship. As time passed, we had both celebrated separately our fifteenth birthdays and as we continued talking twice daily, we became best friends.

After six months and a day or two of developing a serious, friendly relationship over the phone, Hosea wanted to meet me in person. I said, "If my Mother approves, we can meet at our home." Phew, I thought as I stressed, what if he doesn't still think that I'm pretty or as pretty as this Wanda Ruby person he thinks I look like at his school who I don't even know? Nerves set in; nevertheless, I asked Mother for permission to meet him. Upon receiving Mother's approval for his Mother to bring him to our house for a face-to-face meeting, I shook my head and said, "Finally, it's going to happen. 'Then what?" I had forgotten to tell him that I had a family of very protective, curious, and territorial brothers who would be there and that our Mother was a minister of the Gospel. After all, I was only fifteen, did not date, and had never had a boyfriend! Any boy who had ever expressed an interest in me had been beaten up and halted before getting in my space or my face.

Any possible suitors all went to the same school as I and my entire family of school-age youth did. In a conversation between me and Mother, I said, "Mother, please tell Jonathan, Jared, and Jethro not to threaten or, hurt or run him away because I like him."

I was allowed to call Hosea to tell him that I had Mother's approval and gave him the best day and time for the visit. Our first meeting date was scheduled on a Sunday afternoon after my family had returned from church and had eaten Sunday's meal together. He could come at 3:00 p.m.

After he talked to his Mother about the scheduled date, and she agreed to bring him, he called me to tell me it was a go. He said his Mother would drop them off at my house for an hour, then return to pick them up.

"Them"? I was stunned at the idea of him inviting someone else to my house, and I wanted to know who was coming with him.

Well, it was his friend George, my school acquaintance, the same one whom I had passed along my phone number to give to Hosea upon his request so he could call me. I didn't particularly care for or about George and would have never wasted breath to even speak to him. As far as I was concerned, he was an invisible man.

It seemed I was not the only one nervous about the upcoming face-to-face meeting. Hosea was obviously just as nervous as I was. Why else would he bring his friend to my house to see me?

After talking on the telephone every night for six months, we had fostered a seemingly good, friendly relationship. He seemed nice and funny with a likable personality. Finally, it was time to determine if we liked the visual presentations. In other words, he wanted to see if I looked anything like my yearbook photo, and I'd have the same opportunity to see what he looked like in real life. Photographs could be altered. We needed to know whether we could appreciate being in the same space with each other to continue or even decide if we wanted to grow the relationship! The awkwardness was normal, given how we met. The bottom line was that still or frozen photos didn't always provide the real picture; that day would be as if two visually blind people received natural sight.

Anticipation Jitters, Yikes!

Oh my God, the week we had planned our first in-person, face-to-face meeting was almost here, and I was having anxiety attacks one after another. I wondered what to wear, how to style my hair, etc. Then I decided to stop worrying and breathe because we had already been enjoying our telephone relationship for over Six months, so at least we were friends! I always looked at his photo when we were on the phone and found out that he did the same with mine.

   On Sunday after church, I changed clothes. I wore a soft-pink- and-blue-flora front-tie halter top to accentuate the slimness of my waistline and a Bermuda shorts-length khaki skort (skirt) with short tan boots that accentuated the curvaceous definition of two beautifully shaped and toned muscled legs that could have only belonged to a majorette, kickboxer, or dancer. I went for a hairstyle that was referred to as a baby-doll look (cut bangs, sides swept upward) and back hanging just below the lower portion of my neck toward the shoulder line. My only makeup was the new peach-flavored pink frosted lipstick that was no more than a peach-colored lip gloss that smelled and tasted like peach delight candy and a black/brown eye- liner pencil that outlined my eye slant and the lower portion of my expressive almond-shaped eyes. Like any other infatuated young teenage girl, I wanted to accentuate what I felt was my most appealing physical attractiveness.

At 3:00 p.m. sharp, I heard a knock at the door, and my brother Jonathan rushed in front of me to answer it with, "Yeah, what do you want?"

I yelled out, "He's here to see me," as I also screamed, "Mother!" Mother came in as I opened the door for Hosea and George, welcoming them into our home.

I sat between the two young men. I offered them sweet tea or Kool-Aid while enjoying general conversation as we laughed and cracked jokes. I got up a couple of times to get the water they requested but didn't really want as they stared me down. I heard Hosea say, "Well, she doesn't really look that much like Wanda Ruby in person, but she's cute. And wow, she is so fine, my god!" I had to pretend not to have heard them talking as I returned to the living room area.

The hour quickly passed, and his Mother was back to pick them up. We said our farewells, and Hosea said he'd call me later. He did not contact me again for two whole days. This was so uncharacteristic of him, considering the daily telephone relationship that had already been established. I just assumed he was no longer interested. I also knew I had to wait for him to call me since I was a young lady. In those days, girls didn't just pick up the phone and call boys. Chasing after boys was disrespectful and frowned upon. It just didn't happen!

> *"Oh, Give thanks to the Lord, for he is good;*
> *his love endures forever!"* — ***(Psalm 118:1)***

The Question is, Will You Be My Girl?

Out of the blue, he called a whole two days later, I found out and understood that he was just nervous because he didn't know if I liked his visual. He asked me if I liked him now that I had seen him in person, and I said yes. He proceeded to ask me if he could be my boyfriend, and I said yes as long as he understood that I wasn't allowed to go out on dates, but maybe after I turned sixteen in a few months, I might be able to go to a movie once in a while if my family became more familiar with him and trusted him. Still, there were no guarantees because I had a cotillion coming up after my sixteenth birthday that I was readying for.

I would be a debutant, and I hoped he would be my dance partner for the ball. My entire family would be there for my coming out and being introduced to the community as an eligible well-kept young lady. I didn't know if he would continue as part of my life or not, yet I was filled with so much anticipation. I really liked this boy but at the same time couldn't let him or anyone know that!

Mother was okay with me calling Hosea my boyfriend because she knew I would rarely see him because of our distance. He lived in a different district and attended a different high school that was also a rival of the school I attended. We were fifteen, and neither of us had a car or even drove at this time. The districts were a long distance, so there was probably no desire to even think about walking that distance.

Mother also figured a telephonic relationship was perfect to ensure I had no boy interests at my own school.

Sometime during the school year after I had turned sixteen, I applied for after-school jobs and employment where I could work Fridays after school and Saturdays. Old Mr. Freddie Isaiah, the owner of a record shop, was someone who knew my eldest brother, Martin, through the selling of gospel records to his gospel group. He met me at a gospel musical and offered me a job that would involve selling records in his shop. The problem was that his shop was all the way across town in Hosea's district. I accepted the job. One of my older brothers, Jonathan, would take me and pick me up from work for a while. It was just a weekend job on Friday evening from 5:00 p.m. to 9:00 p.m. and Saturday morning from 9:00 a.m. to 2:00 p.m. I quickly had to learn the bus route to get there and return home. Mr. Freddie told Mother that he would ensure that I got to the bus line safely each Friday night and Saturdays in the afternoon.

Hosea got his driver's license and would have liked to have used his mother's car when he could to take me home, but it just didn't work out that way since he had a weekend job as well. His work normally took him out of the area where he played guitar for a couple of singing groups.

At the record shop, fresh old Mr. Freddie was always commenting on my anatomy. I hated that this disgusting pig of a man had to take me to the bus line. He said the nastiest things, and his breath stank as he would try to kiss me and missed.

Hosea would stop by the shop to bring me a sandwich and soda before getting on the road on Friday evenings. Mr. Freddie would get angry each time Hosea stopped by, even though the shop was not busy. He told me, "I don't want your little old boyfriend coming back into my store. He is not a customer, and you don't have time to talk to him when you're here." The next time Hosea came and left, he said to me, "If that boy comes back in here, I will fire you unless you let me touch you and make you feel like a woman! I'm a man, and I can make you feel good. He's just a boy".

Matthew 7:15 describes Mr. Freddie, "Beware of false prophets, which come to you in sheep's clothing, but inwardly they are ravening wolves."

I felt sick to my stomach after he said that, and I thought to myself, if my family knows you said that to me, they will kill you. I chose not to say anything to my family, but I told Hosea what he had said when we talked on the phone later that night. Hosea told me to quit that job.

I said, "No, not yet because I'm saving up to get a pair of shoes that I want, and I need to pay something on a school project."

He said, "I really don't want you working for that scum. You're my girl, and if he touches you, I will kill him! I will be by to pick you up on Friday evening during the time I would normally bring your food."

That's the way it went down, and on the way home, Hosea asked me about the shoes and what store had them. He said he also needed a description of the shoes, the size, the cost, etc. He also asked me how much I needed for my school project. I told him $15.

He dropped me off at home and kissed me goodbye as he rushed to get to work. He always asked me if he could kiss me, and I liked that. He never just took it for granted. We briefly spoke telephonically when he got home from work late Friday night. I didn't go back to work at the music store and had to let Mother know that Mr. Freddy had been very disrespectful and that was the reason I quit the job.

Hosea called and told me to influence Mother to allow him to stop by on Sunday evening to bring something, and I did. He had taken his weekend earnings and purchased the shoes I wanted and gave me the $15 in a note that said, "If you need it and I have it, it will always be yours! You're my girl, and I would give my life to keep you safe and make you happy!"

I felt so overwhelmed by the gifts and his sweetness, yet I could not just accept them without my mother's approval. I had always been told, "Don't you accept anything from no man because there are strings attached".

Hosea respectfully told Mother that he knew I needed these things and wished she would allow me to accept them. No strings would be attached. Surprisingly, Mother told me to accept the gifts and tell him, "Thank you!"

*"And my God will supply all your needs
according to His riches in glory by Christ Jesus."
— (Philippians 4:19)*

Preparing for the Cotillion

The funds had been paid by the parents of this year's debutants who would be coming out during the fall. Monthly meetings and classes and clinics on how a lady should conduct herself in our society were attended. Classes and clinics that taught or demonstrated proper etiquette and displaying of good manners, having great hygiene, dressing for the appropriate appearance, learning to waltz, and wearing that winning smile had become weekly practices by now. Mother had purchased the fabric and pattern for my dress and gotten it to the seamstress. She got my shoes out of layaway so I could take them to the meeting to practice the cotillion dances, how to step up with my parental escort when my name was called, and learning to bow properly to them when I was introduced to the society.

Hosea had made himself available for the final two rehearsals; however, my brother Jonathan kept getting in the way and practiced the dance with me while Hosea sat and waited. Hosea could not make the first dance clinic, so Jonathan stood in his place so I wouldn't have to be there without a dance partner. My entire family knew how sensitive I was about possible embarrassing situations, and I was grateful for my brother's standing in. But now I wanted him to move aside so I could practice waltzing with Hosea. Jonathan is the second of my eldest brothers, and he would be serving as my parental escort if my eldest brother was unavailable.

Phew! Finally, he allowed Hosea one opportunity to practice waltzing and the two-step dance with me, and I was so excited. After the rehearsal, Hosea had to rush out, and Jonathan brought me home.

What is a debutante ball? The following definition and information is from Wikipedia and quite accurately describes what it is. A cotillion or debutante ball in the United States is "a formal presentation of young ladies or debutantes to 'polite society,' typically hosted by a charity or society." The ladies introduced will vary from the ages of sixteen to twenty-one (younger ages are more typical of Southern regions while older are more commonplace in the North). In some areas, fifteen- and sixteen-year-olds are called junior debutantes. To gain entrance to a ball, debutantes must usually be recommended by a distinguished committee or sponsored by an established member of elite society, typically their mothers or other female relatives. Wearing white gowns and satin or kid gloves, the debutantes stand in a receiving line and are then introduced individually to the audience. The debutante is announced and is then walked around the stage, guided by her father or a male representative from her family who then presents her. (This was the South, and the debutantes were sixteen and seventeen years old.) Her younger male escort then joins her and escorts her away and dances the waltz. Each debutante brings at least one escort, sometimes two. Many debutante balls select escorts and then pair them with the "debs" to promote good social pairings.

Cotillions may be elaborate formal affairs and involve not only debs but also junior debutantes, escorts and ushers, flower girls, and pages. Every debutante must perform a curtsy—also known as the St. James Bow or a full-court bow—with the exception of Texas debutantes presenting at the Waldorf Astoria Hotel who perform the Texas dip. This gesture is made as the young woman is formally presented. Debutante balls exist in nearly every major city in the United States but are more common and larger affairs in the American South.

Finally, it was the evening of the debutante ball, and everyone was all dressed up and at the function. When it was my time to walk up as my name was called, both Hosea and my brother Jonathan walked over to meet me. I looked over toward Mother with tears running down my face and said, "Mother, I only need Jonathan to walk me around the court. Make him sit down after that part because I want to dance and sit beside Hosea, not my brother!"

Mother looked over at my brother and said, "Let Hosea dance with her after you march her up there!"

I was never so grateful as Hosea grasped my gloved hand with a smile to dance and sat with me throughout the remainder of the ball. I had finally come out as an eligible and proper young lady going into my senior year in high school. I left the ball with my family. Hosea had to go home alone. Our telephone relationship had developed into a rather serious, old-fashioned, heartfelt, loving courtship.

The pureness and depth of real care and admiration we held for each other could only be expressed as budding love!

"Go to the ant, thou sluggard; consider her ways, and be wise:

"Which having no guide, overseer, or ruler,
Provideth her meat in the summer, and gathereth
her food in the harvest." [She is ever prepared.]
*— **(Proverbs 6:6–8)***

Oh My Goodness, What Have We Done?

The conversation about sex finally reared its curious, probing, anxiety-causing head! As teenagers, both Hosea and India knew that an unplanned pregnancy could cause stress, anxiety, panic, and added expense. Teenagers lack the wisdom of adults. Who would have thought she would conceive on their first sexual encounter? From virginity to being knocked up was a panic attack for India. She did not have the access that an adult female may have had. Every woman deserves access to excellent health care; however, poor people in those days generally were at the mercy of a charity hospital or took chances at the hand of a less skilled person in the home or a midwife who may or may not have had professional formal training in caring for pregnant women and in the child delivery.

There was no confidential provision of services free of charge. A teenager or unwed woman may have had to walk that road alone with little to no help and much judgment, ridicule, and humiliation from others. She was made to feel that she was a disgrace and a disappointment that maliciously brought shame to herself and her family. The girls are always the ones taunted and punished. Society would say boys will be boys, men are naturally dogs, but the pregnant girl is a whore. No female is ready for such ugliness, and I feel sorry for those who suffer society's criminalization of their character. Many poor girls are raped, abused, and or exploited, yet they are all treated the same.

I was not ready for sex, but I loved Hosea with all my heart and knew he loved me, too.

We had been in a relationship for three years, and the first two were mostly telephonic, where we talked two or three times a day. I usually knew when he would call and ensured that I was near the phone. I remember the day he asked me if I would consider having sex, and my first reply was, "What's the rush?" He said, "It's not rushing; we love each other, and since we are engaged to be married, Kitten, I really want to get closer. People who truly love each other have sex, which is how they get closer.

He said, "You are still going to be my wife, aren't you?" I replied yes, and since we will be married for all of our adult lives, I think we should wait. He asked me,

"Why don't you want me completely like I want and need you?" I told him I did, but this was not the right time. He wanted to know when it would be the right time, and I said on our wedding day. He said, well, let's just table this conversation for now and talk about it later. I agreed. After a week or so, the discussion resurfaced.

I told him that I was scared and didn't think I could handle the pain associated with losing my virginity and that having sex would undermine my mother's expectations for her daughter. I did not want to disappoint her in any way. My mother was a domestic worker, unlike his highly educated mother, a full-time registered nurse who also assisted in the work of a midwife. Hosea loved me even though his mother felt his family was better than mine because of her education and professional career. I always knew she felt like that, but that was her problem.

Well, I finally consented to go all the way with my love. He won, I was smitten, he was smitten, and his affection and romantic actions and constant conversation about how much he truly loved me and would never let anything negative happen to hurt me wore me down. He promised that nothing bad would happen, that he would be gentle, and that he would protect me with his life, even from the snarling of his mother. I trusted him because I loved him, and I knew that he loved me, but I was still very nervous and uneasy because God and, my parents, my family would expect me to show restraint. They were hoping that I would be married before having sex.

We were minors, and just because so many other youths were sexually active should not have pressured us as it obviously did him. Eventually, the act was committed, and what a physically painful and messy ordeal it was. Hosea was so apologetic, but that didn't erase my spiritual shame of the act, nor did it dismiss the memory of the physical pain, stress, and visible mess. I told Hosea we would only repeat this act once we were legally married, and he agreed. Sex was not as great as all the hype surrounding it!

One month and a week passed, and I saw no sign of my monthly cycle. I quietly waited in hopes that it would resume, and when Hosea and I talked on this particular evening, I could not hold that bit of news from him any longer. Finally, I belted out, Hosea, "I did not have a period, and it's been one full week past my first missed monthly cycle; I am losing my mind silently." I was so scared. In frenzy on the phone, I asked several times, "What have we done? What do I do?" He said, Kitten stop freaking out!

Crying, "I said I might be pregnant. I have never been late and don't know what to do; I'm scared." What are you going to do to help me? You know I can't tell my family. Oh my God, I'm doomed! Hosea calmly said, Kitten, don't worry, and let me tell my parents. I screamed, "No because your Dad will tell my family, and still, I am doomed!" He said, please stop freaking out, and you're not doomed, we're in this together, I'll handle it."

He called me back and said, tomorrow, before your mother and brothers get home, I'm coming to see you, and we'll work it out. He asked me, "Do you trust me?" I said, "Yes, you already know that I do." He then said, "You know I love you with all my heart, and we're going to be okay. I said, "Okay," hung up the phone and went to sleep.

The following late afternoon after school, while looking out of the window, I noticed his mother was driving, and he sat in the passenger seat. She got out and told him to stay in the car; I heard him say, I want to see her, but she firmly told him, stay!

He obeyed her command as she walked up the two steps to my front door and said, "Get a full glass of water. I did and rushed back to the door. She handed me two large off-white-colored pills and said take this and drink the full glass of water. I took them and drank the glass of water as she watched. She looked at me and said you'll be okay; stop having sex until you are grown! Aren't you a Church girl? Hosea cannot care for your baby, and I will not!' Wow, what a cold-hearted, scary woman she was.

That night, I suffered severe cramping and very heavy blood flow. My mother just thought it was that time of the month. She got up to give me aspirin because she was accustomed to me having cramps during my monthly cycle. She went back to bed when I told her I was okay. I felt like my insides were being torn out, and I saw clumps of tissue and what I thought was flesh mixed in the blood, and it grieved my heart and soul. If you have never aborted your unborn child before, you cannot imagine the personal agony, anguish, and mourning that occurs from within the soul.

Hosea kept calling me through the night, crying and saying how sorry he was that I was suffering alone. I lied and said it wasn't that bad to help him move beyond the guilt so he could hopefully sleep. I dismissed it from my mind and thought of more pleasant things, and of course, we did not repeat the act of sexual promiscuity during our teenage years. Later, I found out that he had been pressured into having sex with me by his older half-brother. When I heard that, I was enraged. We could have waited and not have endured this painful, emotional experience and sinful act of murder.

Nevertheless, we continued to love each other with what appeared to be an even deeper attachment. I learned that it was a bonding of our souls, which became tied together because we had joined physically and spiritually. I strongly advocated encouraging other young couples to wait to have sex until after they say I do. Waiting would make the most positive impact on a relationship. Sex bonds a loving couple together whether they're married or not. I learned that feelings of attachment can last a lifetime.

The Bible warns us about fornication and its potential to hinder our relationship with Christ and harm our souls. My Mother had a very strict Christian Evangelistic outlook on what is knowingly godly and ungodly. I did not want to hear her sermon to me about being an easy target for delving into fornication, nor did I want to have to deal with the shame she might have endured because of my activities. Mother constantly reminded me and other young ladies that we were expected to refrain from sex if we were not married to the young man who might encourage us to allow him to deflower us. She always used me as the young lady whom others should emulate. I hated being the model but was happy about how proud Mother was of me.

My family was very active in church. Everyone knew and appeared to look up to us. The church offered somber admonitions concerning fornication. It taught that girls and boys, especially teenagers, needed to be chaperoned to ensure the temptation of fornication was not acted upon. The subject of teen and premarital sex was ongoing in high school, as boys would prey on girls whom they believed were easy targets. Some students belittled sex, but most jumped at the chance to whisper about it and approach and further exploit girls they had heard were sexually active. People ridiculed pregnant girls, even if they had been raped or abused. God considers any sexual intercourse outside the marriage covenant a severe transgression. Abused individuals are victims, and pregnancy cannot be hidden after a few months. Unfortunately, victims are stared at and categorized the same as submissive individuals.

We were taught that there are dangers of fornication to the spirit, soul, and body, which is why waiting on the Lord for a suitable mate was so important. There are not only physical consequences to fornication but also spiritual damage to the souls of those willing to engage in what is strictly forbidden in God's Holy Word. I honestly did not understand what a soul tie was as a teenager. My mother would tell me and other youth around us that we would leave the door wide open for the devil to move into our lives, giving him a place to set up camp if we were to engage in premarital sex. She went on to explain that not only that but making love to someone means you will be joining your soul to that other person. Even though she described a soul tie, we didn't understand what she was trying to teach us.

Now I know that such coming together isn't under the sanctity of the marriage covenant, and it also leaves the participants wide open for spiritual attacks. The parties unite in spirit, and their souls are bound together as one flesh in the eyes of God. Since our bodies are the temple of God, we defile the temple and become impure when we participate in fornication. The biggest takeaway is that willful sex outside of marriage is sin because it falls under the list as fornication. Sexual abuse is definitely sin and dishonors God. Individuals who do not study the Bible would not know this. I heard it and still did not fully understand, as I should have. Thank God for His grace, mercy, and gift of confession and repentance. His word assures me in 1 John 1:9 that "He is faithful to forgive us of our sins."

I was taught that Fornication means premarital sex, extramarital sex, adulterous behavior, and homosexual activity. These all fall under the umbrella of fornication by the Bible's definition. Any sexual activity outside of God's marriage covenant falls under fornication. Fornication changes lives forever, not just yours but your entire family and even the families of others. Making a sober decision to have sex outside of marriage can lead to unwanted pregnancy, abortion, the onset of an incurable STD, losing the love of your life because of betrayal, divorce, having a child with congenital disabilities, becoming infertile and even demonic oppression, to name a few. These are some of the consequences generally written and spoken of fornication. When people know better, they can do better and stay faithful to God's word about this subject.

If God is tugging at your heart and telling you it's time to stop sexual promiscuity, stop.

My experience with teen pregnancy and enduring guilt of abortion took something away from me and damaged my soul. Eventually, I confessed to my sin of fornication and the sin of murdering my unborn child via abortion. I am grateful that God is faithful and He keeps His promises. I am confident that God restored fellowship with me when I confessed my sins, and now I feel whole again.

"If we confess our sins, He is faithful and just to forgive us our sins and to cleanse us from all unrighteousness" **(1 John 1:9).**

Professing a Love That Stood the Challenges of High School

Hosea and I would talk and hold on in silence together on the telephone for hours during the wee hours of the night until we each snored on our ends of the phones. We discussed everything, even plans for our future. I already knew I'd attend a local university, and Hosea needed to work more with the local music groups and bands to earn money for college or join the military. He had hoped to receive financial assistance through a band scholarship by graduation for us to attend the same university. We attended rival high schools. He was in the marching band for his school, and I was a majorette for mine. Each time our schools played, we didn't care who won. We were just excited to have a chance to see each other. He would come over to whatever sides of the field that my school sat on to sit beside me after the half-time shows were over.

The first time he did it, some of the male schoolmates became boisterous. I stood up and told them to bring it down a notch and leave my boyfriend alone before my brothers dealt with them. After that, we never had any issues concerning his visiting or sitting with me, and he was treated civilly. He always had to change sides near the end of the game to get on his school's band bus, etc.

Hosea chewed Juicy Fruit gum and left me with a quick, sweet Juicy Fruit-gum kiss as he dashed off to the other side of the field.

That's just the way it was, but we would talk later for hours during the night when he phoned me.

Hosea played his guitar for and with outside music groups—i.e., quartets, etc.—on weekends and during holidays to earn money. He was saving money not just for school. On Christmas Day, during our senior year, he came to my home and spoke with my mother first, bearing small gifts. Then he stepped in front of me and said, "I have loved you since before I met you face-to-face." Hosea went down on one knee and took a small box from his pocket with a small diamond engagement ring, and said, "India, will you marry me?"

I appeared shy in front of everyone, but said, "Yes!"

Hosea stood up and picked me up and spun around. He stayed there for a while before leaving to go home to have dinner with his family. I gave him a pair of gloves I had purchased with some of the funds I had received from parents of kids of whom I had written term papers for and a scarf I had personally knitted for him that bore his favorite color combination of blue and tan.

This was quite an exciting Christmas season. I had purchased and sent his mother a set of two floral handkerchiefs. His mother was a nurse who worked a lot. She wasn't particularly friendly to me, but I didn't care because she wasn't my mother. During her off days and holidays, she seemed to enjoy having suppers and dinner parties with her friends at her home. I was never invited nor ever attended anything she had. Hosea was always glad to get out of attending her dinner parties as well. It seemed like she was always trying to couple him off with one of her coworker's daughters who had also attended Catholic school with him when they were young kids. I once received a call from a girl who said her name was Brenda, and she identified herself as Hosea's girlfriend.

I told Hosea about the call while he was visiting me, and he said, "I don't care anything about that girl. I would never give her the time of day, and she knows that. She's one of my mom's coworker's daughters who attended Catholic school with me when we were kids."

He called the young lady from my family's home phone and had her apologize for bothering me and admit that she knew he had no interest in her. I was relieved to have him clear that up because he not only professed his genuine love for me before the masses and placed his ring on my finger but also his love seemed so apparent in how sensitive he was and how he seemed to care about me and anything that concerned me.

I was convinced that I loved this sweet young man as well. After all, I was his girl. We would someday marry, and I would be his wife. When the people he knew would see me and ask, "Who is that?" He would smile and proudly say, "She's my girl, the love of my life."

"If I give all I possess to the poor and give over my body to hardship that I may boast, but do not have love, I gain nothing. Love is patient, love is kind. It does not envy, it does not boast, it is not proud. It does not dishonor others, it is not self-seeking, it is not easily angered, it keeps no record of wrongs. Love does not delight in evil but rejoices with the truth. It always protects, always trusts, always hopes, always perseveres. Love never fails. But where there are prophecies, they will cease; where there are tongues, they will be stilled; where there is knowledge, it will pass away" — ***(1 Corinthians 13:3–6 NIV)***

Pressure Does Not Feel Good and Causes Irrational Behavior

In late April, a month away from high school graduation, Hosea called, and I could tell that he was gravely disturbed. I asked what could possibly have him so bothered. He gasped and said, "My mother is transferring from her job. We are moving to New York the week after my graduation, and I have to move and help her drive and get settled! She and my dad split. She never mentioned leaving before, and I just can't believe she would do this to me and to us. She just doesn't seem to care about how I feel. We need to get married as soon as we graduate so we can stay together. We cannot allow this to separate us."

I said, "Hosea, we're only seventeen years old and are not able to get a marriage license on our own! It is obvious that your mother doesn't want you to marry me, and if we were eighteen, you wouldn't need her approval. Neither of our parents will sign for us to get married. I have already been accepted to and must go to college here." I guess this is how it feels when you're almost but not quite grown yet! "Before we even knew each other, I had always known that I would finish college. Hosea, you know we have to be able to take care of ourselves because I can't imagine us living with your mother or mine."

As the weeks rushed by, Hosea really turned up the pressure to get me to leave with him. It almost psyched me out when he told me, "There are colleges and universities in New York. I can't even rest with the thought of leaving you here when I won't be here! Don't you love me?"

The thought that he was being forced to leave already caused me to feel ill and helpless, and now his desperate persistence for me to elope with him really annoyed and caused me deep anguish. I was beginning to feel somewhat depressed, and it was becoming more and more difficult to hide my depression to the point of speaking out of sorts with my own mother, something I knew better than to do! I whined to Mother, "I don't know why I have to go to school here!"

Mother very bluntly said, "Because you're not grown yet, you're not married, and I'm not signing anything to marry you off because you need to be able to take care of yourself! There is no guarantee that you and that boy will stay together or that he would ever be able to take care of you. I can't let you put yourself at the mercy of his unpredictable mother. You are a very smart girl. I raised you right, and you have a godly duty to do the best that you can, and I'm doing everything that I can to make sure you do just that! Use your common sense, and see beyond all of this. This is just temporary, and after you finish school and get a job and you still want to marry him, do it then. If he can't wait, then he wasn't for you in the first place. Life will still go on."

Graduation day came for both of us and was held on the same day at each of our schools.

My family was in great attendance at my graduation not only to witness me graduate with honors but also to hear them mention that I would be attending one of the local universities next school year.

I had no idea who attended Hosea's graduation, but we did talk and I would continue to go to school there while he worked so I could get a degree for teaching young children.

The best-laid plans don't always come to fruition! When the fear factor set in, faith in the plan seems to dwindle, dissolve, and dissipate.

"If any of you lack wisdom, let him ask of God, that giveth to all liberally, and upbraideth not; and it shall be given him"—**(James 1:5)**.

"For the Lord gives wisdom; from His mouth comes knowledge and understanding"—**(Proverbs 2:6)**.

Hosea came over so we could spend time together as we only had a few days before he would be leaving for good. We needed to have a heart-to-heart talk and figure out concrete plans if there was to be a future for us. We parted with the plan of him moving and getting settled while I started college as originally decided, but once he was established with a local band to begin banking money, then I would join him immediately. By that time, we would both be eighteen years old, and I would have completed my first semester of college. We would go to Las Vegas and get married, return to New York. I would continue to go to school while he worked.

When Dreams Change and Directions Differ, Two Cannot Walk in Agreement

I had a vision of my life being married to a musician, and screamed, "Oh god, I'm scared!" I knew that could never be my life based on what I had heard about musicians' indiscretions and partially due to my own childhood of having a father as a musician.

My father was a musician who also played guitar just as my fiancé did. It seemed he only came home to shower, shave, color his hair to hide the gray, and dress to go out and play in clubs and cabarets. During the weekdays, he worked in his mechanic shop; after all, he was an A-1 mechanic and the proprietor of his own business. Because of his many indiscretions, that man had so many children with numerous women (his "groupies"). Who could possibly keep count? He had eight children with my mother, although one of my older brothers died as a very young child. My dad had children being born during the same years that I and my known siblings were born; he had children being born by younger and younger women each year. I heard there were thirty-nine children accounted for, but only God knows. He used to practice on his guitar and teach my second oldest brother how to play, and that brother taught me and my younger siblings how to play little runs to songs such as "Peter Gun." I heard that our dad was an awesome musician and that women were crazy about him. They were his groupies! He was an attractive man as well who could not stay faithful to any woman.

I had very little respect for my father growing up, and I had decided in my mind after listening to well-meaning family members that my fiancé might turn out to be that same kind of husband and father to our children should we have any. The thought of living that familiar old pattern of loveless and disrespected existence scared me immensely. I and Hosea would never be able to walk in agreement if his future behavior mirrored the lifestyle of my dad. Had he been allowed to stay in Macon, Georgia, to acquire and aspire a higher education instead of being made to move away with family and thrust straight out on the streets to seek employment, using his already-great music talent and experience, we may have had a better chance of anticipating a successful marriage and life together.

Upon arriving in New York, Hosea contacted me to say that it was beautiful and unlike anything I had ever seen. He could hardly wait until I got there so he could show me around. After a month passed, he called to say that he had some information for me from well-known local universities, and after finishing my degree, I could teach school while living in the house with his mother until we were able to afford a place of our own. All I could do was scream under my breath, "Oh no!" I and his mother did not share a kindred spirit, and I would never live under the same roof with her.

Each week, the pressure from Hosea was mounting. Not only did I feel stressed about his constant badgering for me to join him there, but as I examined my dreams for my life and possibly a missed opportunity for living within my own personal goals, desires, ambition, and purpose, I was also completely torn in two.

I pondered what to do when paths that started together forked or diverged. Here we were at a proverbial life's standstill in our relationship because we both had our own God-given purposes that would cause us to move in different directions; however, both of us wanted to hold on to a piece of that romantic thread of the past, yet neither of us wanted to give up our path to walk the other's path. Hosea felt he knew what was best. He would pursue his music career, and he wanted me to be an elementary schoolteacher if I felt I just had to work. I had my own dreams, and teaching little children would have been my last option if at all. I thought, What should I do? I could clearly see that we were at a place where our goals were seemingly incompatible. I was haunted by the question of whether preserving the relationship was more important than the commitment to myself for living out my own purpose. I understood that sacrifices and compromises could lead to commitment, but when I thought of my childhood and the less-than-tolerable relationship with my dad, I just could not and would not decide to commit at that crucial and present time. I knew that this was a serious fork on the road of our young lives. Decisions must quickly be made and honored. I felt the pull to select a new destination. Although my emotions flooded inwardly with so much love, my heart ached with having to make what I felt and knew was a common-sense decision and not a heart one.

Too often, distance relationships suffer to the point of an unrecovered status or end. I knew without a doubt that Hosea loved me, and I loved him. Yet he began to feel that I just didn't love him enough. It wasn't that because as I thought and focused on him only, he still made my heart skip a beat.

However, the distance and having to deal with local and home discouragement that was only made to benefit my well-being took an emotional toll on my trust in our relationship's strength and longevity. During excess periods of longing for Hosea's presence, my teary eyes and heart were constantly reminded of Alfred, Lord Tennyson's "In Memoriam A.H.H." The quote simply states,

"I hold it true, whate'er befall;

I feel it when I sorrow most;

'Tis better to have loved and lost, Than never to have loved at all."

I tried little and subtle ways to get Hosea to start thinking about other destinations that would involve his compromising toward my desire, but all he felt was manipulation and betrayal. He was a musician, and he wanted me to have faith in his gift and ability, to support him, and just be there for him. Finally, after almost four months of bickering and feeling badgered, I just told Hosea that I no longer wanted to move to New York and felt we should just put off our marriage plans until I finished school where I was. I tried to get him excited about the new possibilities of me becoming more marketable through my education while he pursued his music career.

He just wasn't accepting my attempts for compromise as he still wanted to stay with the original plan, and I was suddenly at an impasse. I mailed my engagement ring to an address I had received from him, in hopes that it would reach him. If we had continued to argue about our future and how to make it best happen, neither of us would have ever reached our personal destinations. I only wanted him to see reason so neither of us wasted energy by being rash.

I just didn't have enough faith in myself or Hosea to try both of our desired plans—first, going ahead with the original plan to join him, to marry right away, and pursue a local school for a while or agree to allow myself to still join him. The visions in my head began to look bleaker. I refused to be the baggage that would hold him back, so I put my foot down and chose the education I and my parent knew was best and wanted for me. Truth is, at this time, I just could not see myself living the life of a musician's wife even though he felt he could take care of me, whether he made it big or not! Another thing is I am so ambitious and was raised by an independent woman to be an independent woman. As much as I loved him, I don't believe that I could have ever adapted to being taken care of. Truly, that was something I would have had to learn how to do.

I knew that our desire for a life together had probably ended, yet we still loved each other. I also knew that if we were never able to communicate and devise a probable plan, both would just have to live with the consequences of the choice to live separate lives.

I told someone of our plight and stated that without a shadow of a doubt, I knew he truly loved me with all his heart. I blindly loved him too. He loved me so well. We were good together. However, I knew when it was all said and done; it was time for us to move on. I've heard it said that there are just some places you're not meant to go and vice versa! Even if he didn't realize it, I knew I couldn't really go.

Closing a door may not feel good, but one must do the right thing. In this case, it was closing the door on this relationship to allow us both to move on in the fulfillment of our purposes. Unfortunately, we lost communication, but the relationship was never truly severed. I desired to free him so he would not only live but hopefully soar! Most folks have heard the old saying, "If you love something, set it free. If it comes back, it's yours. If not, it was never meant to be."

This is not a description of fate, and most people don't really believe in the psychology of determinism.

That old saying is just an old saying needing no misplaced interpretation about destiny! Any sustaining relationship requires work, commitment, and tenacious communication, having nothing to do with blind fate and destiny!

*"Can two walk together, except they be agreed?" — **(Amos 3:3)***

*"For I know the plans I have for you," declares the Lord, "plans to prosper you and not to harm you, plans to give you hope and a future"— **(Jeremiah 29:11)**.*

Embracing One's Purpose Equals Success, but What About Getting Closure?

Wow, it is such a great feeling to be able to live in your purpose, and it was my desire for both Hosea and me to do just that. In my way of thinking, my thoughts were that we may not be meant to live a life together; but thanking God simultaneously, we could both enjoy a measure of joy and success as we thrived in our chosen occupations or, better than that, our life's callings.

Within five years of our relationship's communicable end, Hosea had been blessed to perform as a member of Barry Manilow's orchestra and for over ten years. He had been traveling as a member of the orchestra, performing in countries and states all over the globe. I finished school with a Bachelor of Science degree in public communication and a minor in secondary education and also entered into military service as a human resource professional. I accepted a federal government job in human resources management as an intern leading to a journeyman and senior-level analyst, which enabled travel and relocation stationing for me from Washington, DC, to countries and towns all over the world while working on an advanced degree. We both obviously loved our work and were tremendously rewarded in so many ways. Hosea had moved away with his family in 1967. The last time we had spoken was in early 1968. My sister Joya and I saw him at a concert where he performed in late 1975 or early 1976, just over eight years after our marriage plans had been disrupted and we had seemingly accepted our alternative lives apart.

Upon finding out about the upcoming concert, I was so excited and really wanted to see and talk with Hosea again, so I had Joya to make herself a new outfit and get two tickets so we could attend the concert. We went, and I saw him after the concert ended. It appeared that Hosea was still very much put out with me, yet he wanted me to hang around and wait for him after the concert, so I did. He made me wait for almost an hour before coming out as I sat near several members of the same orchestra.

His first remark to me as he looked upon me was, "Why are you wearing that wig?"

I replied, "Because I got all my hair cut off. Would you like to see it?"

He replied, "Yes." As I lifted off the wig, he screamed, "Oh no, why did you get your hair cut off like that? I don't like it. It makes you look like a boy."

I thought that was a cruel jab. I tried to ignore his meanness and held my tongue as long as I could, but finally, I said, "I don't style my hair for you, mister. You should have figured that out by now!"

That only fueled his anger, and he wanted to hurt me with words as he pulled and tightly gripped me by the arm while staring at me with those serious, piercing eyes. He pulled me to him. He was so wired and full of contempt that he just would not stop with the mean little verbal pricks and attacks, yet he wanted me to stay and not pull away from him. His interaction was ambiguous at best, and his tight grip was hurting and frightening me.

I felt as if during this moment of anger, I was being treated like an object to be toyed with or an unappreciated groupie whom he was detached from as opposed to his long-lost beloved. My pride, ego, and immaturity did not accept that well, so I retaliated by lashing out in return by saying, "I married someone else instead of you!" I knew that would slam his ego, then I said to him, "Get over your- self." I told him that I wasn't his groupie and did not particularly care for his music and had purposefully stayed away.

I also said that I was very happy for him in his apparent success, but he needed to grow up.

With tears running down his face, he lashed back with something uglier about my actions being disgusting to him, and the smirk on his face showed he was still extremely upset with me after almost eight years. He wanted to punish me to make me feel his pain. He felt I had betrayed him and maliciously crumbled his ego as a man! He said to me, "You threw us away and dismissed me like garbage, like something horrible and unlovable, when you knew our love was real! You made me feel like nothing. You left me waiting at the altar alone. But I'm okay, and I'm going to make it!"

I looked at him once more and said in my laconic manner, "Good!"

One would have thought that as well as he appeared to have been doing in his occupation and career, he would have been less bitter, but it was apparent that he still could not shake our separation and obviously undesired breakup! Yet I never said to him, "I don't want you." But I did say, "You're overreacting!"

Breakups and separations are never easy. They always leave a painful sting. In fact, it hurts both parties immensely. The glaring looks on his face; the sharp, pungent words used; and sarcastic attitude directed toward me revealed the scorn he still felt and his over-sensitive and vulnerable state! Hosea cried out, "Kitten, don't act like that!" I looked at him through teary eyes and open contempt and said, "I have to go," as I jerked away, removing myself from his stinging grip.

I rushed away without looking back. If he wanted to humiliate me, he had accomplished it publicly as far as I was concerned. Under my breath, I murmured, "Goodbye forever, dude. You will never ever see this girl again."

As I rushed away, I thought to myself that this chapter in my life was finally at a close as far as I was concerned. I recalled hearing someone say that "there is a thin line between love and hate," and finally, I felt I understood that cliché. Yet deep down inside, I still loved him very much. I would rather be set on fire than to ever admit that to him!

I was determined to never let him know it because I was indeed settled in my thinking and was moving on. John Steinbeck quotes in his book The Winter of Discontent, "It's so much darker when a light goes out than it would have been if it had never shone." I certainly could agree with that!

*"A soft answer turneth away wrath:
but grievous words stir up anger"* — **(Proverbs 15:1)**.

Release is Not Always Instantaneous, Is It?

Hosea had always been so sweet, caring, loving, protective, and gentle to a fault almost with and concerning me. I had been his sweet, fragile little baby doll, and he desired to take care of me for the rest of our lives. He truly loved me and was in love with me. He affectionately called me Kitten.

The day of the concert, on that very day, approximately seven years and ten months after our official parting, he seemed rather cold, mocking, humiliating, violent-tempered, and apparently unforgiving, scorned, and damaged and angry. I thought this would have given me the closure I needed to truly embrace my freedom and release without remorse and regret, but it did not seal the exit spiritually or emotionally right then. As I met back up with Joya, I said to her, "Get me away from here, and I will never ever see him again. I'm done with this. This was a mistake! Let's go!"

Joya, asked, "Aren't you going to at least stay a while and just talk to him?"

I looked at her and belted out, "No. 'Get me away from here' now!"

We rushed away from the area and entered Joya's car and exited. I had no appetite as we stopped by a fast-food restaurant to eat. I just wanted to go home.

I stayed with my family until the next day, and then boarded a plane for my return home to DC.

Home alone, remembering the encounter between me and Hosea, I thought out loud, "How dare I show up face-to-face and unannounced after all that time had passed, announce myself, and approach this man as if I had nothing to do with hurting him. How pompous to accuse him of overreacting! Why could I not just shrug off his harsh words and piercing stare when I could visibly see that he was still vulnerable, hurting, and shaken? How dare I handle anyone with such self-righteous indignation! The truth remains, as I thought, he still had my heart, and I still had his. Our earlier life's plan had been ripped apart years ago, but obviously, a flicker still remained, and we both had to get beyond this point to find a bit of happiness in others since we could not change our past nor return to yesterday. Too much time apart without communicating and now too much hurt had scared and damaged us for life, and what's sad was he probably didn't even realize it.

 I know that being laconic is normally bad because it just sounds rude to be so abrupt with people; yet I had mastered that behavior and ruthlessly directed it at Hosea for hurting me spiritually and physically during our brief encounter after being apart for so long! I wanted him to still just swoon over me, take me gently in his arms, and say, "I'm just glad that you're here now." That did not happen. As I recall, he felt the need to reprimand me harshly in public. Since he hadn't been able to catch up to me years earlier, his wounded pride needed to show others how strong he was. Of course, I retaliated because I could give as good as I got. He just had never known that side of me. I knew exactly why he was so upset; after all, I was the one who ultimately decided not to join him, break off the engagement, and ignore his calls for weeks on end at my family's home, pretending to be gone. He left a couple of telephone numbers for me to call him back and the times he would be available awaiting my call. I felt stressed out and pulled in two different directions. I thought that I had been very direct and adamant as I told him to stop calling so frequently. I threatened that if he didn't stop calling so much insisting that I give him a date or timeline of when I was coming to New York, I would never join him.

 Truth is, I said he had to stop trying to reach me so much because I couldn't concentrate on my studies, and I had promised I would get with him when I could. Somehow, I didn't think he would really stop calling totally. I thought he would still actively pursue me, no matter what my attitude was or the expense incurred, even if it was sporadically once a month or at least once a year so we'd know how to reach each other and maintain a somewhat-active relationship.

Truly, he was a gentleman, afraid that I would never join him if he didn't ease up on calling and harassing me about a day that I would arrive to stay with him. He made up his mind that he would not budge until I said okay, I'm on my way. All he needed was that small glimmer of hope that I still wanted him and had still planned on joining him. His sudden lack of persistence made me able to move on much easier. The last time we spoke, I told him he would not be able to reach me at school. Of course, changing my phone number to reflect the school administration's office number only deferred the inevitable.

Thinking back on that concert evening's end when I told him my last name had changed for a brief period but after an annulment, I retrieved my maiden name, I saw visible hurt, anguish, full-blown contempt, and disgust for me on his face, his eyes, and his demeanor. I had blatantly blared out, "I got married to someone, and it wasn't you!" I slammed his ego into the ground. How dare I taunt him or anyone like that!

I will never forget how he screamed out, "What?" and he grabbed me, saying, "Kitten, a promise is a promise. How could you just give yourself away to a stranger when you had to know I was still waiting for you?" I felt his emotional pain and knew he really wanted to chastise me when he grabbed my arm in a tight, choking grip and raggedly spoke out at me, saying, "How could you do that? I thought I could trust you! You could trust me! I remained faithful to you! I'm disgusted. I proposed to you and put a ring on your finger because I love you!"

Suddenly, I felt fear, and thought to myself, Oh, Lord, this was a mistake, and I've gone too far this time. Lord, please help me get away from him before he hurts me! Dear God, please let me get out of here safely!

Here we stood before a few members of Barry Manilow's orchestra, and I was so embarrassed and ashamed. He made me feel like a convicted felon whose life's sentence should be commensurate with a heinous crime. I wanted to vomit as he used a razor-sharp voice when speaking before; he violently grabbed me close into his arms. I thought that he was going to smother me publicly as warm tears flowed down his face. He kissed my face and violently kissed my mouth so hard that my lip started to bleed as I tried to pull loose and get away from him.

If I could have made myself disappear, I would have. Although he loved me and could not imagine losing his little kitten, he clearly wanted to punish me for hurting him, stepping on his plans for us, and for damaging his ego. I wondered if I had caused him to inwardly become an aggressive, violent beast. I sure hoped not! I had been the love of his life, and I knew it! He was the love of my life too, the one who made my heart skip a beat whenever I allowed myself to think about him! Oh, but we do make choices in life, and some folks can move on to other paths easier than others. Sometimes we must accept that our paths have already been planned by a Being greater than ourselves.

I heard that he appeared to be having a difficult time entering and securing a meaningful relationship with another woman because he couldn't stop comparing her to me and what we had shared. He just couldn't seem to accept her and that relational situation for what it was. Unfortunately, he had lost his trust and courage to move on. His heart still wanted his imagined sweet little kitten, his porcelain baby doll of a fiancé, India. He was shocked and awestruck by the side of me that he did not know, that feisty little ball of dynamite that had stood before him, yanked away and left him standing alone.

Success in the workplace cannot possibly heal a wounded soul. I stood, thinking in the quietness of my townhouse that I should have never sought him out after so long and so short of a time to plan my entrance back into his life. I was selfish as I felt unfulfilled and really wanted to see and talk to him to assess whether I had made the right decision. I knew he still had my heart because I still missed and loved him so much, even though life went on in his absence. I am not easily stifled! I don't shut down in the absence of people or situations. I always find ways to climb up and out and succeed because I was created that way. Each person needs to know and understand themselves. I know myself, and I knew that the focus and drive inside me serves to catapult my plans and goals to higher heights according to God's will for my life.

As I reflect on that evening with Hosea, we had no privacy; therefore, we could not talk to each other, so we talked at each other in arrogance. Hosea was still bleeding in his heart, and to witness the entire scenario caused me great anguish and feelings of guilt, remorse, and the need to ensure that, that painful chapter of my life was permanently closed. I knew

I had to truly release him from my mind and shield my heart this time. I had to forgive and release myself forever! I could only talk to God about this situation and pray, asking Him for forgiveness and mercy to put this chapter of my life away for good. I asked the Lord to take good care of Hosea as I wanted him to finally heal and move on with that very personal part of his life beyond just existing.

I became engrossed in my work and was finally able to truly move on as God is merciful, healing, and very kind.

When I think about him, I never said, "Hosea, I don't want you anymore, and I'm never going to marry you." But as I ran away without looking back, I just assumed that he would come to that conclusion, move onward with his life and fill the void.

"Brethren, I count not myself to have apprehended: but this one thing I do, forgetting those things which are behind, and reaching forth unto those things which are before, I press toward the mark for the prize of the high calling of God in Christ Jesus".
(Philippians 3:13–14 KJV)

Ghosts Can Haunt Us Sometimes When What We Need is Quiet Relief

Hosea died several years ago, unbeknownst to me, since we had not communicated in over forty-two years. The news of his passing was not 100 percent certain as I also heard that one of his close family members said he had been ill and had almost been lost. I wanted to believe that he was still alive, so I sighed and exhaled with relief. Initially, the news hit me like a ton of bricks and caused me to grieve and, with great urgency, pray for his well-being. I had been completely caught off guard and so surprised! We somehow rarely think about the mortality of human beings', and when it's someone you love, you never really think of them going so far away as death. When I received the news that someone only thought he had died, his death was not real to me. I dismissed my grief as quickly as possible because it had not been confirmed, and of course, I didn't want to believe that he had passed. This time, even though it had been several years ago that my mind had been confused as to whether he was alive or had passed away, it was finally confirmed, and I felt devastated to hear it and barely able to hold my composure. I still loved him even though I had been blessed to live a wonderful abundantly fulfilled life. In fact, life had gone on with little to no thought of him because he was not one of my current or major life's concerns but rather an ancient history of love that had been unspoken of, a relationship that had become inactive and placed on hold—an unfinished business! I felt stricken with guilt and a lack of closure!

After several years passed, my brother, a fellow musician who also lived in the same city as Hosea, had recently lost his lovely, sweet daughter. I and my other siblings traveled to be with him in hopes of bringing some bit of comfort during his period of bereavement. He was grief-stricken and struggling with his loss. We, his siblings, felt a desire and need to accompany him as he dealt with it.

When something as sweeping as death happens, it is so easy to lose your balance. Your life's routines can get skewed, causing people who are left to mourn, to get lost in the swirling vortex of hyped emotions internally, and outside of themselves. And it's not just their own emotions but also from other people's emotions. After reading all the texts and Facebook messages shared by my brother Jet, we decided to be there for him because that's what caring family members do! He will miss his child and will always love her, and we believe and even know that she loved him in this life and kept that love for him with her as she transitioned. The activities they shared will always be a reminder that she lived and loved him. Although she is physically no longer here to share that space with her Papa Bear as she lovingly referred to him, he will miss her dearly but will always be able to cherish the time they shared.

This visit to New York was my first time ever going there. My mind pondered over the ghosts of so many years past when Hosea and I were just seventeen years old, so in love, engaged, having youthful discussions, and making plans for a future together, him having to move away with his mother and me having to stay behind to go to school and having made promises of joining him as soon as I could.

"For the perishable must clothe itself with the imperishable and the mortal with immortality. When the perishable has been clothed with the imperishable, and the mortal with immortality, then the saying that is written will come true: "Death has been swallowed up in victory." **(1 Cor. 15:53–54)**

Once I decided that I could not join Hosea in New York, I declared that I would never go to that state because of our personal history, infrequent communication and, eventually, broken relationship and determination to move successfully into a future that would inevitably shut out the past. Now here I was in this famous city with siblings and other family members of my niece. Immediately after the service, two of our siblings left to return to their out-of-town destinations while I and several others remained and toured the city's many beautiful, interesting sites and cultures that were melted into that region.

During the general conversation, we reflected on the people we grew up with as kids and how so many of them and others we once knew were no longer among the living.

My brother Jethro (Jet) said, "India, did I tell you that Hosea died?"

I reminded him that he was not certain when he mentioned it before, so I chose not to entertain or accept that thought.

He said, "Well I now know for sure that he is dead! Girl, that dear brother loved you until the day he died. He passed on some years back, and it was finally confirmed by musicians who were his close friends." Jet only mentioned Hosea because of our former relationship and him knowing that Hosea never moved on. He strongly believed that Hosea's lifelong love for me was the cause of his inability to move on into other meaningful and lasting personal relationships no matter how many short flings he may have encountered in that wild musician's environment, I know that I always had his heart. Hosea never married or had his own family. Jet mentioned that they used to meet socially with other professional musicians and mutual acquaintances regularly for years, and when he stopped seeing him, he inquired as to his status and welfare. That's when he was informed by one of the musicians who used to play in the same orchestra as Hosea that he had passed. Additionally, another friend they shared confirmed that he was deceased.

Jet reflected on the many past conversations they had, had and how Hosea would say he loved me with all his heart and that he would forever wait for me because there was no room for anyone else. He would tell most people he encountered about me and how I was the love of his life. Jet was introduced as someone who was supposed to be his brother-in-law. Jet said he had even written a sweet instrumental tune/melody that he called by my name. The other musicians who heard the tune used to say, "Wow, she sure must be sweet." He would reply, "She is!"

For some reason, my hearing of his death again and now because of the confirmation felt like it had just happened, so this time it was real for me. I felt like I had been hit by a ton of bricks and momentarily being suffocated. I remember grieving over Hosea and our torn relationship when he first moved away. During that time, we were so young. Now knowing that his life on earth was over, I felt faint, and yes, I mourned him deeply because not only was he my first love, the girl he gave a beautiful engagement ring to who had said, yes, but also, I always knew that, that love was real. As I listened to how he had hung on to the ghost of an old but true love relationship we shared throughout his entire life from when we were young, my spirit was sorely vexed. I thought on his sweetness, and it caused me to mourn a life whose joint plan with me was stunted before it actually began due to a purposeful divergence. I know that God has a plan for every soul that is born into this world, and each must live out their purpose and return. As I reflected over and over, I had to remind my mind of that truth. The mere thought of him being dead and the knowledge of us having unfinished business made me "puke" and scream out of a feeling of guilt, remorse, and regret! Suddenly, I thought of that Mariah Carey and Boyz II Men song, "One Sweet Day." The song says,

> "Sorry I never told you all I wanted to say…
>
> And now it's too late to hold you
>
> 'Cause you've flown away so far away
>
> And I know you're shining down on me from heaven
>
> Like so many friends we've lost along the way and I know eventually we'll be together
>
> One sweet day…"

Of course, we know that God is love, and in heaven, love is pure. And we shall receive the light of His love and reflect it all on the Lord, our Creator, and our King! We will again rejoice with loved ones who have gone on before us, and what a day of rejoicing it will be for those who accepted Christ as Lord of their lives.

As I think about it, our adult life together did not manifest, and obviously, it probably would not have ever been realized due to my lack of trust, personal/selfish ambition, and fear of unwanted possibilities that being the wife of a musician might have brought. More importantly, it was obviously not in the will of God who loves us both equally!

Most long-distance relationships end after a brief period. Ours would also not have stood the test of time due to the abruptly broken relationship caused by such a long distance. This huge physical separation for a time led to poor and eventually nonexistent communication between us. Good constant communication and commitment are necessary for any relationship. The hearsays and the "what if" possibilities haunted me as a possible reality, which betrayed my trust and scared me into not pursuing the chance of what may have been a wonderful and meaningful life together with someone I loved so dearly. We did not have mobile phones, apps, and computers back then. Long-distance calls were expensive, and we shared phone lines called party lines. The thought of separation already felt like a recipe for doom to me! An out-of-the-area move had such a drastic impact on any relationship back in the day, so I made my unshared choice. My guilt-ridden grief was because of these things:

1. I felt I had left him hanging and let him down because I felt I would hurt him if I said goodbye.

2. The thought that he may not have enjoyed a wonderful and fruitful life as I had was very hard on me and makes me sad.

3. I didn't want to think that he had passed away thinking and believing that this life was all there was (the end of his existence).

4. Maybe no one shared with him that God loved him, and that He proved it through Jesus His only son's death on a cross at Calvary, and about His glorious Resurrection by God to His eternal life is real and must be believed and accepted by him so he could live on in the Heavenly dimension eternally.

I remember that he was brought up in Catholicism, and my family and I were Protestants, so we never attended church services together during the time that we courted. He did not attend worship services and I never heard him speak of God!

I didn't think I could have ever let my mother, a strong evangelist, find out about his denomination. I was afraid she would say I couldn't see him because of our belief differences. As I think about it, she probably would have tried to get him to accept Christ as Savior and get him converted, but I never shared that information and I'm sorry about that.

His father was a Christian and a strong believer in Jesus Christ, and Hosea sometimes played for groups in gospel church environments as well as blues in secular settings. Now I'm hoping that someone took the initiative to talk to him about the Gospel and his eternal destination. I pray he had accepted Christ as his personal Savior.

5.   And just like Hosea loved me, even though I moved on with my life, I obviously never stopped loving him on a deep, soulful level. Had I reached out to him earlier and humbly repented for how I left him hanging with the promises I did not keep to join and marry him, he may have accepted my apology and moved on in his personal life. The grief I felt may have been diminished, or perhaps the feeling of guilt would not exist. Holding on to the past often skews everything in our lives from our relationships with other people to our relationship with God. We are all ultimately responsible for the choices we make. I prayed and asked God to forgive me, and I know He has.

I researched and found out that while there was no special or significant other in his life, he had enjoyed a wonderful, purposeful, and fulfilled life through his music career and had many wonderful friends who shared his profession. And I thanked God for that. God is so loving and awesome, He took a little country boy from Macon, Georgia, and blessed him to play for the big-named professional music artist Barry Manilow in the big city of New York. Hosea played and toured as a member of Mr. Manilow's orchestra all around the globe. Upon confirmation of his death, I prayed, hoping he did not go to hell. One day, during my period of fasting and praying, the Lord gave me a vision. He showed me that Hosea had accepted Him as his Savior and was absolutely accepted by Him among the beloved.

In a vision while praying, I saw him looking back at me, smiling, as he walked up a long, high spiral stairwell that I equated and surmised as being the King's Highway. He looked like the picture of health and appeared to be so content. Our eyes met, and I saw what I would describe as pure, genuine love. Suddenly, I felt a bit of release, a knowing that he was finally at peace.

"To everything there is a season, and a time to every purpose under the heaven:

A time to be born, and a time to die; a time to plant, and a time to pluck up that which is planted;

A time to kill, and a time to heal; a time to break down, and a time to build up;

A time to weep, and a time to laugh; a time to mourn, and a time to dance;

A time to cast away stones, and a time to gather stones together; a time to embrace, and a time to refrain from embracing;

A time to get, and a time to lose; a time to keep, and a time to cast away;

A time to rend, and a time to sew; a time to keep silence, and a time to speak;

A time to love, and a time to hate; a time of war, and a time of peace.

What profit hath he that worketh in that wherein he laboureth?

I have seen the travail, which God hath given to the sons of men to be exercised in it.

He hath made everything beautiful in his time: also, he hath set the world in their heart, so that no man can find out the work that God maketh from the beginning to the end.

I know that there is no good in them, but for a man to rejoice, and to do good in his life.

And also, that every man should eat and drink, and enjoy the good of all his labour, it is the gift of God.

"That which hath been is now; and that which is to be hath already been; and God requireth that which is past". (**Eccles. 3:1–13**, **15 KJV**)

I remember a quote by Junot Diaz, author of The Brief Wondrous Life of Oscar Wao, that made me both reflect and hold on to a minor regret and self-sympathy. The quote says, "He was the kind of boyfriend God gives you young, so you'll know both love and loss the rest of your life."

Hosea lived out his true calling of making beautiful music in this life on the earth, and when he reached completeness, the Lord called him home. Life could have faked us out if we had let it. We were meant to meet and share only a brief yet beautiful and important part of our lives in a close Romeo-and-Juliet-resembling loving relationship. It was our youth that was exclusively ours as designed by God. We were meant to grow up and out to fulfill the purposes for which God created us. Life did not fake us out because the Lord was ever in control.

I did learn important lessons such as praying without ceasing to know God's plan for your life; love well and deeply the person God blesses you with; don't be afraid to mobilize to soar in your profession and calling;

listen for the Lord's voice so you do not mistakenly follow the wrong voice; and lastly, know that God does not make mistakes—men do!

The writer C. S. Lewis, in his book A Grief Observed, reminds us that the Lord never promised us a trouble-free life in the following quote:

"We were promised sufferings. They were part of the program. We were even told, "Blessed are they that mourn," and I accept it. I've got nothing that I hadn't bargained for. Of course, it is different when the thing happens to oneself, not to others, and in reality, not imagination'.

We are to leave the past in God's hands as we must walk in the present and live out the purpose for which He created us.

I am convinced that life is a gift. It is short, and it is a vapor as the Bible describes it. We are to live a good life, being thankful daily and enjoying the blessing of each brand-new day, living each day thankfully and gratefully and not living in the past or taking life for granted.

We are to live for Christ, our Creator and Lord, as we strive to live in peace with everyone, we find more love, joy and patience. Make every effort to live right as we live in love, making the most of each opportunity and using our time wisely so we live our lives in the peace given by God. I accept this as the quiet relief we need.

"This is what I have observed to be good: that it is appropriate for a person to eat, to drink and to find satisfaction in their toilsome labor under the sun during the few days of life God has given them, for this is their lot. Moreover, when God gives someone wealth and possessions, and the ability to enjoy them, to accept their lot and be happy in their toil, this is a gift of God. They seldom reflect on the days of their life, because God keeps them occupied with gladness of heart" —
(Ecclesiastes 5:18–20 NIV).

From the Desk of the Author

When something as sweeping as death happens to someone you personally know and there are unresolved issues that you just never took the time to deal with, it's easy to lose your balance and get lost in the swirling vortex of heightened emotions that are inward and outward. You have to deal with it, especially when some level of guilt and remorse is felt. You need God's forgiveness and blessed assurance that all is well, and you must get to a place where you can forgive yourself for the sake of release and closure.

Some folks will want to know why in the world would I write a book about someone dealing with ghosts from their past. I always counsel young folks, encouraging them to leave the past in the past as it is not their present. Truly, I live by that same counsel; but in some cases, we all have to deal with obviously unresolved emotions that we didn't even know or had forgotten were there. Psalm 139:23 says that the Lord can search us and show us what is hidden in our hearts, allowing us to repent and be forgiven: "Search me, O God, and know my heart: try me, and know my thoughts:"

Through prayer, the Lord gives us the closure we sometimes never even realize we needed. In Kelley Armstrong's book The Calling, we can agree with her quote, "Remembering or Forgetting, I'm not sure which is worse."

I maintain that we must still get to that place where we can leave the cares of loss and guilt in God's hands and move on. It's true. I have suffered enough loss that by now, I know enough about it and realize that you never stop missing someone you cared about. You allow God to fill that huge gaping hole of their absence.

If you've ever caused anyone hurt or pain in this life, you need to confess it and ask them for forgiveness while they are still living if that is possible. Next, ask God's forgiveness, and learn to forgive yourself. If you neglect this necessary life link, you are sure to some- day feel great remorse that seems to be so much worse should the individual pass away before you've asked for forgiveness. Once they're gone and you never took the time to ask for forgiveness, anyone who has a heart and a conscience automatically feels guilt-ridden.

Mitch Albom, in his book For One More Day, asks the following question, which is also an idea to ponder and consider the effects on one's life, "Have you ever lost someone you love and wanted one more conversation, one more chance to make up for the time when you thought they would be here forever? If so, then you know you can go your whole life collecting days, and none will outweigh the one you wish you had back."

Gail Caldwell suggests in Let's Take the Long Way Home that "we never really get totally over great losses; we absorb them, and they help to carve us into different, most often kinder, creatures."

I like this idea, especially knowing that the Lord uses everything to work for the good of those who love Him and are called for His purpose.

Criss Jami says, "Listen to God with a broken heart. He is not only the doctor who mends it, but also the father who wipes away the tears." This is what I believe!

God is so merciful and will allow you to research His Word and meditate on it, review media, receive visions, and write out your resolve to move beyond it so you'll never have to deal with the object of each painful personal subject or experience again. He will enable us to be able to help others and understand how to receive closure in similar areas if they need it. He is also a God who will allow you to love again if it is in His plan for your life.

My answer to the question of why I would write such a book is simply this: I am a writer, a human being, and a highly sensitive person and simply an empath. I feel everything deeply daily, and I aspire to live in my God-assigned purpose and calling as He uses me to help in even some minute way of "kingdom building."

Understanding that everyone has a purpose to fulfill, I made a decision that allowed me to live life on purpose and accept the side-bar consequences of my actions with God's help.

One reason some people don't discover their God-given dreams and life purpose is that they don't stop long enough to survey the obvious. They just don't listen.

We not only encompass our lives but also touch the lives of others. It's so easy to lose your way, so there comes a time when we must be still and listen to what God is saying to our hearts. He allows us to make choices. Events will occur that help to steer us onto the right track as He orders our steps in His Word when we ask Him to.

"Be still, and know that I am God." (Ps. 46:10)

To know our purpose and receive vision from God, we need to be quiet and hear Him speak to our hearts. We must hear Him, receive the vision, and not become discouraged when our well-expected life plans change because we are now focused on our real purpose. Those who listen and grasp the vision can see it and can live the real dream as they thrive in God's purpose for their lives.

I hope this story will not only touch your heart, encourage you, and remind you that everyone over a certain age has a past. Additionally, it provides insight on how to deal with past haunting issues for receiving the closure you must have. It helps you to know that you don't have to get caught up in chasing after ghosts, hoping to obtain release and ultimately relief for living the remainder of your life in your God-given purpose.

Finally, I must agree with the author Paul Coelho's quote in Eleven Minutes,

"Anyone who has lost something they thought was theirs forever, finally comes to realize that nothing really belongs to them. No one loses anyone, because no one owns anyone. That is the true experience of freedom: having the most important thing in the world without owning it."

So, we conclude that Hosea and India did not truly belong to each other. Their lives in the past and the paths lived out by each of them all belonged to the Creator, God. The loss of anything you once held very dear to you or anyone who meant something special to you will hurt, no matter how long it has been since you've thought about it or communicated with that dear one. It is the kind of pain that won't feel real at first, and when it does, it seems to take your breath away. Only telling God about how you really feel and allowing Him to help you get beyond what has passed will help! He's able to help you come to terms with any situation and get you past your feeling of guilt!

Unforgiveness is not an option, so we forgive and ask God to forgive us as we also forgive ourselves, leaving the past where it belongs and aspire to flourish in this life and the present.

Elizabeth Gilbert, in her book Eat, Pray, Love, reminds us that "it all goes away. Eventually, everything goes away." But God's love is everlasting, eternal love!

"As for man, his days are as grass: as a flower of the field, so he flourisheth.

"For the wind passes over it, and it is gone; and the place thereof shall know it no more." (**Ps. 103:15–16**)

The first time I read those two scriptures, I cried because it's so true. One exposition basically explains it this way: When we meditate on and read this passage over again, we find in the history of man that as he lives out his little day, he is cut down at last, and it is far more likely that he will wither before he comes to maturity or be plucked away all of a sudden, long before he has fulfilled the time he planned on living. It's God's plan and the timing He has allowed that really matters.

"As a flower of the field, so he flourishes." He has a beauty and a certain comeliness even as the meadows have when they are yellow with the kingcups, but alas! How short-lived. No sooner come than gone, a flash of loveliness, and no more! Man is not even like a flower in the conservatory or the sheltered garden border. He grows best according to nature as the field-flower does, and like the unprotected beautifier of the pasture, he runs a thousand risks of coming to a speedy end.

Thank God that our Lord is eternal and everlasting because this means He exists outside of time. He observes all events throughout our history as if they are simultaneous. He alone can do this because He is God.

We don't know what our lives' future holds, but He does! God knows what our future holds without affecting our present or our free will. This story of how life almost faked out Hosea and India was merely a human's perspective since God is timeless and can observe the entire course of their history all at once, the same as a person might observe events along an entire course of a highway from a mountain all at once. The takeaway from this amazing yet seemingly sad but successful story is a reminder that God knows everything, and He's ultimately in control.

He doesn't make mistakes; we do. That's why we should accept and trust Him because we were made for His purpose. It is He who knits every part of our lives together for the good and His glory. He knows what is best for us!

When He sent our little souls to live in the form of fleshly human beings on the day, He gave us to be born, He also knew the day we would die and when our spirits and souls will return to Him. We are all given a purpose and a time to accomplish it; therefore, I encourage anyone and everyone I encounter to live your life's purpose on purpose and do it well to the glory of God!

"Many are the plans in a person's heart, but it is the Lord's purpose that prevails."— **(Proverbs 19:21)**

About The Author

Victoria Robertson was born and lived in the States below the Mason Dixon Line. Although she is a new author, she is not new to writing and the arts. Her love of artistic expression and literature comes from her upbringing in a city where music and history invoke love and expression in many forms.

She believes the whole world is her stage and she can make any location her home. Victoria wants people to see the world through her eyes because she can see the sunshine on even the dreariest of days.

Love, art, passion, and creativity make Victoria Robertson an amazing and captivating writer. She hopes to show others that it is never too late to live out their purpose.

Printed by Libri Plureos GmbH in Hamburg, Germany